where

are the love poems

for dictators?

*The numerous tyrannies on our
continent have never had a writer
worth mentioning on their side.*

Isabel Allende

where

are the love poems

for dictators?

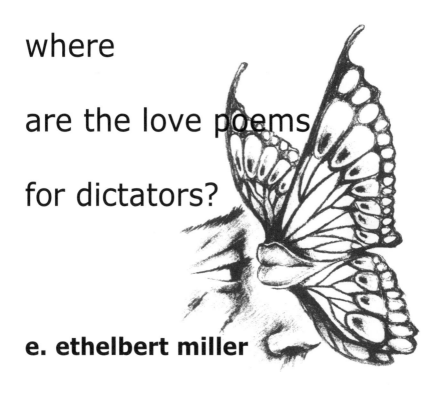

e. ethelbert miller

with a new introduction by John Cavanagh

illustrations by carlos arrien

OPEN HAND
PUBLISHING, LLC

Greensboro, North Carolina

© **1986 and 2001, E. Ethelbert Miller**

OPEN HAND PUBLISHING, LLC
P. O. Box 20207
Greensboro, North Carolina 27420
336-292-8585 / 336-292-8588 fax
E-mail: openhnd1@bellsouth.net
www.openhand.com

Design and production:
Deb Figen, ART & DESIGN SERVICE
3935 South Findlay Street
Seattle, Washington 98118
e-mail: artdesign@jps.net

Library of Congress Catalog Card Number 2001 132681

ISBN 0-940880-65-2 (paperback)

SECOND EDITION
Printed in Canada
05 04 03 02 01   6 5 4 3 2

Acknowledgment is made to the following publications in which some of these poems first appeared:

Ariel
Blind Alley
Callaloo
Chile Alert
City Paper
Footwork '85
Genetic Dancers
LIPS
Montpelier Plus 4, 1980-1984
9-1-1 Hotline to Contemporary Culture
Race Today Review
Reflections
SOL
Sojourner
Visions
Whose Woods These Are
Working Cultures
World's Word

in memory of Richard Miller

contents

Introduction

As humanity crawls out of its bloodiest century, there are rays of hope. Chilean strongman Augusto Pinochet, who overthrew a democracy to create a human rights nightmare, gets arrested on two separate continents. The first arrest in London earns the ailing Pinochet the nickname "the English Patient." More importantly, it opens a door to the heretical notion that dictators might be stripped of their immunity from prosecution for crimes against their own people.

Through that door, pursuers of justice spring forth in surprising places. A Chadian dictator, with the blood of tens of thousand on his hands, is arrested in Senegal. Others prepare cases against Pinochet's soul mates in Paraguay, Surinam, Guatemala, and Argentina. There are even stories that Henry Kissinger has quietly declared a moratorium on overseas travel. A dictator, Pinochet, becomes a verb: to be "Pinocheted" — a future that any past or would-be dictator now must ponder.

Flash back two decades. E. Ethelbert Miller, magic pen in hand, guides us through the lands of the dictators — an all too recent chapter in human history that the media has closed and declared gone. Sketching vignettes of the Cold War, these poems haunt us with the bayonets and blood and prisons of Chile, El Salvador, South Africa, and Beirut. They inspire us with those who would throw the dictators out of Nicaragua.

In the midst of Ethelbert's lyrical travels through dictatorships and revolutions, the institute where I work — the Institute for Policy Studies — was struck by Pinochet. IPS had hired one of Pinochet's arch foes, Orlando Letelier, in 1974. Letelier had been a minister in the democratic government that Pinochet overthrew, and he quickly emerged as a visionary opposition leader and perpetual thorn in Pinochet's side. So, on September 21, 1976, agents of Pinochet detonated a bomb under Letelier's car as he drove to IPS with two co-workers. Letelier died a brutal death along with Ronni Karpen Moffitt, a young employee at IPS. The day that horrible international crime was committed, several of my colleagues announced their suspicion that the pursuit of justice would lead to Pinochet and that very day, they announced their determination to seek justice in this case.

One of Ethelbert's 1983 poems, entitled "day of protest/ night of peace (for chile)," opens with these words:

> "when the generals invite you home
> do not salute them
> when they ask you to forgive them
> do not forgive them"

Ethelbert wrote these words at the height of Pinochet's powers. Seven years later, the dictator would negotiate his way out of the Chilean presidency by forcing his opponents to make him Commander in Chief of the Army and a Senator for life. The deal was struck: Pinochet steps down but receives immunity for life. Or so he thought.

Thousands in Chile, the United States, Canada, and Europe pursued Ethelbert's words: "do not forgive them." At IPS, we worked with so many others to press a legal case to send the two generals under Pinochet to jail for the killings of Orlando and Ronni. In 1995, we won round one as the two generals were convicted in Chile and sent to their own private prison. We worked with the brave Spanish lawyer, Juan Garces, who survived Pinochet's coup and never forgot. On behalf of thousands of victims of the Chilean dictatorship, Garces initiated the legal proceedings against Pinochet, insisting that dictators are not immune to prosecution for crimes that violate international law. And so a once mighty dictator was placed under house arrest in London.

The twin arrests of Pinochet in England (1998) and Chile (2001) are testimony to persistence in the struggle for justice, persistence by Chileans, by Spaniards, by my colleagues, and by people from all over the world united in common pursuit of justice. This persistence is a story which must be shared far and wide.

And now, we move to a new phase in this work, the phase of giving life to that new verb: to be Pinocheted. We understand that this is a global struggle and we salute the human rights movements and lawyers who are using the Pinochet precedent against human rights abusers from Chad to Paraguay, from Guatemala to Argentina.

Ethelbert's poems also remind us of some urgent unfinished business as the new century turns our gaze toward the prospect of some justice for the world's poorer majority.

Lurking in the shadows of these poems is the nation that armed and fed and clothed the dictators: the United States. In 1984, Ethelbert writes "thriller":

> "america
> falls in love with michael jackson
> & no one is curious
> about CIA involvement in central
> america"

He ends the poem:

> "america remove your sunglasses"

Perhaps the next step is to remove our collective sunglasses and examine the bloody history of the U.S. government writing love poems for dictators. What about a truth commission in the United States? Perhaps it is finally time.

Elsewhere in "thriller," Ethelbert intones:

> "tonight
> maybe for katharine hepburn
> & the girls in the balcony
> we should stop and examine history
> before it's too late"

Ethelbert opens this book with the words of Isabel Allende: "The numerous tyrannies on our continent have never had a writer worth mentioning on their side." Our side has E. Ethelbert Miller. He is not only one of America's great contemporary poets. He is a teacher, an activist, an organizer, a great humanitarian. He serves on the Institute for Policy Studies Board of Trustees, and he has read his poems at memorial programs for Orlando Letelier and Ronni Moffitt.

Feast on his words.

John Cavanagh
Director
Institute for Policy Studies

3-30-01

The Institute for Policy Studies is based in Washington, D.C. (www.ips-dc.org)

I. days of protest/night of peace

juan

i meet juan
at the outskirts
of our village
we say nothing
walk to the water
where boats sleep
stuck in sand
we push one forward
into the smells of morning
check our nets
as the sun looks through
the openings in heaven

senor rodriguez

the old truck creaks
to the side of the road
victor the driver says we have to walk
the last miles to the fields
senor rodriguez refused to fix the truck again
he is an old man who sleeps with his money
now that his wife is dead
there are 12 men in victor's truck
another 30 somewhere in the dust ahead
we all carry machetes
the inside of our hands hard like the earth
we live on
our shirts hang from our chests like leaves too
tired to fall
i listen to victor curse the truck
the way i do the sun and senor rodriguez
in the middle of the afternoon
when sweat runs like rivers down the muscles
of my back and i have only prayers
to count the hours

juanita

when she was small
she wore the lipstick of her mother
face made older with powder
like the pictures of movie stars
cut from magazines
the blonde ones she taped on the wall
next to jesus

madonna

four children on a blanket
eight children in a room
i sleep with my eyes open
the belly of jose swollen
like a half moon
there is no milk in my breasts
to comfort his needs
yesterday miguel walked to the city
to beg for food
it was his birthday
i had no gift
i prayed that Miguel would not steal
the soldiers wait in doorways
they bring us bullets

church of god

today we held mass outside the church
there are hundreds of people
women & children
ramon tells me they come
from the countryside
he points to where the sun
rests in the evening
smoke in the distance

i place my hand on ramon's shoulder
i instruct him to prepare
the church for the people
the war is young
i hear babies crying
my prayers wait for answers
tonight i will write a letter
to the government
i will light the candles
on the altar

jerusalem

who is this man they call fidel
whose face is everywhere
why is one man blessed & cursed
   by so many

driver

i came to the city
about three years ago
& found work near this airport
business is good here
especially since the war

newspaper people
come from north america
i know them by their clothes &
poor spanish

they pay good money just to see
the mountains & the countryside

when they ask me questions
about communism or the government
i smile & say

   pete rose/pete rose

sometimes they laugh
sometimes i laugh

we seldom
laugh together

el salvador

the soldiers march through the streets
like the beads of my mother's rosary
i count them
i lose count
i count again
i am not afraid of dying
so much death i have seen
the grass red
the flowers red
the rivers the color of blood
there are fingers where leaves once floated
there are flies fasting from too much flesh
when peace returns
this land will be filled with farmers not funerals
i swear it
mother of god

near the old indian ruins

near the old indian ruins
i walk with the ghosts
of my fathers
i hear the old songs
the thunder in the wind

out of this earth
will come a giant
a god for the holy

the holy who walk barefoot
the holy who cannot read
the holy who have no food or land

out of this earth
will come a giant
a people united
standing proud and tall
beneath their feet
will be the ashes
of this world

untitled

when i heard my first bomb
i thought it was the earthquake
the noise broke the large jars
& the fences where mama kept
the chickens
i was very much afraid

in the early days
there was little resistance
planes flew deep into the mountains

my father was killed around
the time i was ten
i remember the year we buried him
it was a year for death

one could always find bones
growing in the fields

she wore a red dress

in salvador
there is talk of elections
but rumors travel like death squads
the shadow on the corner is not a man

in the morning
i see bodies
lying on the ground
like discarded bottles and cans

in the afternoon
everything is normal
streets are crowded
children return from school
mothers shop
young girls flirt
with legs miraculously
scarless

in salvador
i am constantly
looking over my shoulder

it has nothing
to do with beauty

traveling
in
central america

if one
is a visitor
   a stranger
        or both

one
is
always   cautious
    of cars
    empty streets
    soldiers
    children

even the american embassy

roberto

in chile
maria
holds
roberto
in her hands
in her hand
a photograph

gone
is the
laughter
& the smile
of our friend

when
i ask
the authorities
about roberto
they shrug
their shoulders
they say
they have
not seen him

they ask
is he
missing

between
life & death
there are only
pictures

when allende was alive

looking through the window of my country
i do not see myself outside
i trace the outline of my breath against glass
the cold enters my fingers

when allende was alive
i could open this window
look out across chile from my home in
santiago

there were no curtains to hide dreams
it was a time of hope

a time to press democracy against my lips
& hold her like a lover

carlos

maria
collapsed
by the tree
in the yard

her tears
told us
the news of carlos'
death

      i asked
      for his
      body

      &

      they
      laughed

      they told
      me i could
      have it
      if i paid
      for the
      bullets

      what
      vultures
      rule this
      country

holding
maria's hands
my mother
softly whispered
to me

juan
there are pesos
in my room

por favor

there is a place
where the sea goes
when it is tired

last week we marched to the square
to protest the shortage of food
we were women not politicians
we were mothers not communists
we were thousands not hundreds

it made no difference

bayonets and blood
they beat us
clubbed us
opened our stomachs
with knives

they told us

do not worry
about food

the dead do not starve

untitled

where are the love poems for dictators
i sit on a stool in a small room
no windows
i can touch walls without moving my arms
the smell of myself eats the last slice of air
in this prison
the food is terrible
it is a tasteless horror
in the next cell antonio weeps
his body already crushed by a thousand burns
at night i whisper poetry through the cracks
in the wall
my words like women kiss his eyes

day of protest/night of peace
(for chile)

when the generals invite you home
do not salute them
when they ask you to forgive them
do not forgive them

there are too many missing graves
so few flowers left
there are families and bones broken
scattered across this land/world
where we live

when they invite you home
do not try and take all the things
you have found here

no

return home with all that you left
if only the promise to return
is all you took

from the diary
of a young revolutionary

april 18th

      in every land there are whores
      and rulers who are whores

      and who we love
      is often what we love

so you ask about nicaragua

several days after somoza fled
i left the house of a friend and
went outside to take pictures of the stars
it was the first time i noticed them

thriller

it's close to midnight
& america wonders why michael jackson
wears one glove
while in argentina jews are missing
& the coast of nicaragua
is surrounded by mines

america
falls in love with michael jackson
& no one is curious
about CIA involvement in central
america

michael jackson turns into a monster
& ronald reagan becomes teddy roosevelt
the whole western hemisphere
is westside story

tonight
maybe for katharine hepburn
& the girls in the balcony
we should stop and examine history
before it's too late

america remove your sunglasses

postcards from miami

from the restaurant we could see
the hotel that survived the earthquake
further proof that this country
needed us   what could one buy now
except cheap jewelry and the latest
fashions from eastern europe some
of us who stayed after the revolution
slept with postcard pictures of miami
over our heads   there are no clubs and
the movies come from cuba   still we meet
in the afternoon to drink and remember
the good days   the beer is warm and the
wine expensive   the good stuff was gone
long ago   like lucille ball we try to
laugh and convince ourselves that life
too is filled with reruns

war on columbia road

when the woman
pulled her clothes
from the hot dryer
i saw the burns on the
backs of her arms
scars sticking out from
beneath a short-sleeved blouse
as she folded
shirts and towels
i knew the skin on this woman
had been changed by bombs and torture
not by accidents
which claim their victims
in kitchens

after the generals

there are new slogans in the air & on the walls
i watch my mother at work in the kitchen
she is learning slowly how to read
slowly stumbling out of the past
now & then she rests her head on the table
the pages of her notebook filled with promises
my mother can spell and read so many words
she tries to read the newspaper everyday
& everyday she has questions

how long will this revolution be?
when will we have more food?
why was manuel killed?
were not things better under the generals?

questions
& more questions
& questions i cannot answer

what do i tell my mother
a woman with so few tomorrows

how much forgiveness remains in her heart
& after the rule of generals
what is left to forgive

poem #1

if i had a pass
i could watch the
sunset in johannesburg
instead i ride the crowded
train
the hot smell of my brothers
mixing with the dust
the coming blackness of the
night
moving along the track

nicaragua

what can i give you nicaragua
tears or blood
should i embrace you like i would
another man's wife
the shape of your back curving
against my hands
the brown earth color
of our meeting
on this loveless night

nicaragua
i have known prostitutes
i gave them money
now i look into the eyes of honduras
and costa rica
behind the headlines that hide behind
lies and something called america
a fruit filled with bones

nicaragua
if i never see the sun again
i will count your lovers among the
many that defended you
i will remember you dressing in the morning
near the window
i will remember your voice
and the way the wind carried your song
into the mountains

nicaragua
this poem is for our children
and your friend in managua who asked
me to live with her
whose face i wrapped in tissue
her hair like fine black thread
covering my shirts

this poem is for the poets
who will understand

the homelands

it's always hot
on the day the men return home
the heat coming from their bodies
fire so bright
it burns the sky over
johannesburg

untitled

beirut
like when the new york
yankees terrorized the
american league
the tanks of israel
push back the palestinians

outside lebanon
no one asks for
autographs

untitled

when there are no more poems to be written
go & wake the dead
tell them that the war is over
that victory is ours
tell them that the living too
have found peace

poem for marucha

when kisses find their wings
they will return to our lips
to fly again

II. dead flowers

another love affair/
another poem

it was afterwards
when we were in the shower
that she said

"you're gonna write a poem about this"

"about what?" i asked

poem

let me die at 33
like john reed
a witness to revolution
& his own turbulence
i want to be the man
you know by name & reputation
not by touch

art is a long way
from this moment

if i didn't make up these poems
would you believe my life
the emptiness so rich it overflows
with loneliness   who are you
but a woman who walks inside her
own mystery   whose love is so
external it describes only gestures
you are the dream that did not last
the night   i am the man whose face
you will remember when your husband
returns from his affairs   let my
poems console you   here is the
pain i felt when you left

playoffs

while i watch the playoffs
you use my phone to call
some other man

you stay until
the fifth inning
then say you have
to leave

i watch you exit
like a pitcher heading
for the showers

somewhere someone
is keeping score

you perfect your game
with each man

love is the best curve
a woman can throw

dead flowers

dead flowers are omens like dust comin up a road to
     swallow rain
don't you take nothin like that from no one she said
she gave me the eye that years ago i remembered
     meant that a whippin
was comin and i would have to hold back every tear
     and drop of pain

uh huh i said she gave it to me outside church
said it died cause of the heat but you know i think it
     was dead
when she picked it or either it died from the pickin
what you think momma

you askin what i think son   you don't want to hear
     what i think
i think that girl's evil
devil done kissed her spirit and loved her soul
wouldn't let her kind come near my house
and if i was you i wouldn't have nothin to do with her

women like her take everything they can take
leave you naked in their bed or in the street
it don't make no difference   they don't believe in
     right and wrong

your father he almost got caught by a woman like that
second year we married he start comin home late
don't want me to do nothin but cook
he didn't even touch me in the middle of the night
so i know somethin wrong and somethin not right

and one day i catch her holdin his arm downtown
so i knew what i felt all along was real and
what i saw was more than i could feel

your father he don't see me cause that woman got his
        eyes
she holdin them like a snake before it bit
she got his eyes real good but me i knew i had his heart

and i come home and find the things your grandma left
things some folks don't believe in anymore   things
        they say don't work
but you know son evil don't change   so the old
        ways is still good

i know evil when i see it and i saw it then
just like i see it now   you holdin a dead flower in your
        hands

so i fix somethin to fix this girl
not to harm her but to set her straight
to let her know i got the power and she be wise not to
    touch my man

and you know that same night he come home whistlin
and he take me in his arms and i whisper—thank you
    jesus

and after we love and he sleep and i rise
i remove the dead flower from his bible near the bed

s'cuse me while i kiss the sky
(for lady j)

so she said to me
she said:

some men will pass thru the gap in your teeth
walk down your tongue
and sit in the back of your mouth
flashing a flashlight down your throat
in search of promises and their own failures

for every man there is a woman
and for every woman there is loneliness
walking down the street on a sunday morning
holding a cross in one hand
and a child in another

every easter i have watched women
in their best clothes
standing in front of vacant apartments
believing in the resurrection of old neighborhoods
and saturday night lovers

it is a question of faith
either you believe there is a man waiting for you
or you believe you are waiting for a man
it is a question of faith

the young woman waits for joseph
the old woman waits for jesus
it is a question of faith

she told me this
she said:

s'cuse me while i kiss the sky

thulani

girl
what you do is your business
who you love or who you want to love
does not set the sun in my life
there are enough miracles for everyone
girl
i wish you happiness
like a nice home in the country
good playgrounds & schools for your kids
i hope they even learn a second language
& translate neruda from english back to spanish
girl
when that man comes along
& tells you that you are like poetry
that in your eyes are all the things he ever imagined
ever wanted
ever needed
never/never mind about what you're gonna wear
just dance with him into forever
girl
don't let no one tell you it ain't time
especially when the fever you have
calls your man doctor & the medicine
is so good you know you can't be well without it
girl
take it & keep it with you
always

two women: or a conversation with sahara nile

you need a change she said
why with horses dying in new york city and all
you need to leave this place

you need to find a small town out west
somewhere where a man can be a man
& women can be what they want to be

when i first needed it
lord—can't even remember
but then when was the first time
you made love to a woman you really knew
& could remember her first name
as well as her middle initial &
other things most private

why i bet you never held a real woman
like me in your arms
look at you
you look like you looking for something
& not even god know what it is
& you too dumb to ask for help
i tell you
you better stick your thumb out
& listen to miss sahara nile

why with horses dying from the heat & all
you don't need any more signs to tell you
love is difficult these days

now i love myself
& never loved my lovers
cause i love the truth more than i love a lie
now some men will warn you
before they harm you
the ones i know will simply ride you
until you die

we need a change she said
& she put her arms around me

mississippi

death surrounds itself with the living
i watch them take the body from the house
i'm a young kid maybe five years old
the whole thing makes no sense to me
i hear my father say
    lord jesus—what she go and do this for
i watch him walk out the backdoor of the house
i watch him walk around the garden
kick the dirt
stare at the flowers
& shake his head shake his head
he shake his head all night long

yazoo
jackson
vicksburg
we must have family in almost every city
i spent more time traveling than growing up
guess that's why i'm still shorter than my old man
he don't like to stay in one place much
he tell me

soon as people get to know your last name
seem like they want to call you by your first
boy   if someone ask you your name
tell them to call you mississippi
not sippi or sip but mississippi

how many colored folks you know name mississippi

none see

now you can find a whole lot of folks whose
name is canada
just like you can find 53 people in any phone book
whose name is booker t. washington

your mother she was a smart woman
gave you a good name
not one of them abolitionist names

what you look like with a name like
john brown or william lloyd garrison
that don't have no class

your mother she name you after the river
cause of its beauty and mystery
just like my mother named me nevada
cause she didn't know where it was

only language
can hold us together

only language
can hold us together

i watch the women
bead their hair
each bead a word

braids becoming
sentences

she would
never comb her hair
it was always wild

like new poetry
it was difficult
to understand

she would enter rooms
where old women
would stare & mumble
& bold ones would say

"where's her mother"

she never understood why
no one ever understood the
beauty of her hair

like free verse
so natural as conversation
so flowing like the french

or spanish she heard or
overheard she thought she knew

"i want to go to
mozambique" she said one day

combing her hair
finding the proper beads
after so long

"i want to go to
mozambique" she said

twisting her hair
into shape the way her
grandmother made quilts
each part separated &
plaited

"i want to go to
mozambique or zimbabwe
or someplace like luanda

i need to do something
about my hair

if only i could remember

the words
to the language
that keeps
breaking in my
hands"

grenada

near the beach
grenada enjoyed taking long baths
instead of quick showers
she would mix her oils & select
her soaps depending on her mood

grenada would comb the sunlight
from her hair every morning before
she dressed

the clothes she wore were colorful
oranges & greens/yellows & blues
around her neck grenada wore her
precious jewels

jewels her neighbors
found room for in their gossip

"where grenada get dem things
she poor as we
& she think she something
she think she big u know"

& grenada would laugh
wonder to herself why people were so jealous
& quick to judge

so grenada went looking for someone
she could share her time with
someone who could understand
what she already knew—the joy of being free

outside her village
grenada found her friend
an old woman who lived in the mountains
where spanish hung from the branches of trees
where the rivers were named after jose marti

the old woman called herself cuba
her mother's name was angola
her grandmother's egypt

so when grenada went for long walks
she headed for the mountains
she would walk barefoot along the narrow roads
her feet barely kissing the untouched earth

grenada would always find cuba
planting something in the small garden
beside her house

there

the two women
would sit for hours
surrounded by trees/birds/plants/flowers

"once i almost lost this"
cuba whispered to grenada

her voice
so soft
the wind stopped to listen...

& once
when grenada left cuba
it was dark
the way back to the village
seemed too far to walk

she knew
someone was following her
she ran
her jewels falling to the ground
as she stumbled

then the night engulfed her like a hand on her throat

&
cuba could be heard crying
in the mountains

arnae's jazz

like new music
friendship never
grows old

just a kiss in the dark

nothing makes sense
especially the women i've known
i should have kept a diary
or started writing science fiction
but i fell in love
with movies
and people who say the right thing
at the right time but always leave
i wanted someone to say something
wonderful or maybe
just hold me baby just once
i've always kept my promises
even to women who loved women
and never loved me
i never wanted to be lonely
no one ever does
i only wanted the popcorn
not the kisses in the dark

stephanie

you start breaking promises
and you'll begin keeping secrets
now my daddy never spoke much
he was always tired from working
or just had nothing to say   i'm
thinking about him in the middle
of this argument since she found
out i've been sleeping with stephanie
and all she wants to do is pack a bag
and get the hell away from me   we both
sitting on the bed   she crying and
i'm trying to keep something together
that i've just taken apart   all the
time i ain't said a word more than
my daddy

when nightfall comes

tell me when nightfall comes
when the day is over
& we can see the stars
the closeness of our hands & hearts
joined in such joy
let us call it magic
& be surprised
that this discovery
our love
was never seen
before

tao

the
woman
who calls
herself
a buddhist
follows
me
home

poem written on the 4th of july

& if i did leave
where would my leaving take me
into last week's argument or
maybe the first night we made
love

this is for the moment:
the making of a wrong turn
the asking for directions

III. poems from blue mountain

blue mountain

blue mountain got its name from the blue people
who came from the middle of the lake
looking for food on the shore

finding nothing
they sent prayers up to the sky
in the form of clouds

a few clouds
got caught near the top
of the mountain

struggling to free themselves
they slipped and fell back into the lake

if one wishes
to see god
one must look through water

the poet who came to live
by the lake

after the great war
artists who belonged to the new order
returned to the country

here they lived without dreams
dedicating their entire lives
to their work

one poet came to live by the lake
near the blue mountain

here he planted poems
that became flowers

these flowers were scattered
across the world replacing
the ones picked by ghosts and widows

untitled

when
you're
small

white
folks
always

want
to touch
your head

for
good
luck

elaine beckford

when the dog needed walking
we would walk the dog
out near the river where the johnsons lived
and the rich folks had summer homes
and maybe a few of us like ginger and eddie
would toss rocks into the water
take our shoes off
splash each other and try to scoop
small fish up with our hands
our world was perfect
like sunlight coming through the curtains
and finding a special spot on the wall or floor

i never had goosebumps until the summer the
body of
elaine beckford was found in the water
near the big rock and police came and told my
daddy
to keep us indoors and it was three weeks later
that they shot a colored man
a few miles from where we lived

some of our neighbors said he was innocent
but most people said he was only colored
and someone had to pay for doing what they did
to elaine beckford   let it be the colored
my daddy said and no one knew but me
that my daddy was real sweet on elaine
and i caught them twice together in the barn
she no older than i
and i don't even know what they doing
cause i ain't old enough to know

sarah

whistle blowing like a train coming down a track
quitting time and me and sarah
walk to our lockers where
i got my friday night dress already hanging there in
        the corner
sarah she so tired she forget what day it is until i
        remind her
that tomorrow johnnie suppose to be coming back
        from the service
and since the war been going on there ain't been too
        many folks coming back

something tell me that johnnie won't look the same
willie next door to me come back with one leg and a
        flame
in his chest that keep him coughing all night
sarah she love johnnie so much you just mention his
        name
and she pull them letters out that everyone done
        seen almost
at least three times   i'm her best friend so i've seen
        them
and lost count   they all come from paris and she
        got a big
rubberband holding them together

one of the girls don't know where paris is
but she knows it's a little further than fort charles
that's where they keep the men until they ship them
        overseas
after that half the girls in the factory might as well call
themselves widows   kiss that new home good-bye
        and pray they
ain't got a child they got to raise by themselves

as soon as the men board that boat
i watch some of these girls counting the days on them
church and drugstore calendars
and the ones that stop counting begin to look a little
big around the waist
i tell sarah she should be happy johnnie coming back
half a man is better than no man at all
don't take no war to make you understand that

the kid

about the second month of the season
we start catching word about the kid
talk about strikeouts and shutouts
how his curve breaks and his fastball smokes
frank and i were driving trucks up in the mountains
listening to the games
betting our wages and drinking beer
we get the newspaper each morning
and check the standings
frank is a giants fan
been that way since the day willie mays broke in
that was the same year his father died
in an accident on the highway
three days before christmas
sometimes when we ain't talking about baseball
frank will talk about his father
talk about him the way some folks
be talking about the kid

clement sitting by the bar

i ain't ever fell in love with no singer
never was a woman who after she sang
i wanted to fall asleep inside her voice
you know—wait until she got her head back
and her eyes closed—a soft embrace
stretching from her lips to someplace behind
her heart—no i ain't never felt that way
about no one   come close now and then
especially when i was in the city
but i'm not a real music lover
never loved no singer
anyone who could sing about leaving a man
will give you a hard time
and anyone who just by opening their mouth
can put a warmth between your legs
is gonna give you trouble
i've been sitting by this bar for a long time
and i've seen a lot of guys tapping their feet
when millie over there sings
now that woman can sing some blues
make you cry and make you mean
loving millie is like taking your first drink
you get it down and it opens your eyes
and then you say you want some more
before you know it you either sick or drunk
i picked a lot of guys up off this floor
and most of them was crying over millie
no i don't love no singers
and i only have a drink now and then

michael ray

wake up with joe louis
hittin me in my stomach
ribs hurt so bad i can't rise
mama sittin in the chair by the window
i look at her and know i'm not gonna make it
she rockin there the way she did
when aunt mae died
mournful rockin like it ain't got no purpose
just keeps goin back and forth
guess when you have ten children
some gonna be here longer than others
you just accept that and keep rockin
no fault but mine that i was drunk
and couldn't stay on the road
wake up now and my life done gone
wish i could get out this bed
and kiss that woman
god i love her so

tyrone

nothin like the smell that comes from fresh cut wood
i like workin with my hands
buildin and takin things apart
when my daddy was alive i was always in the toolbox
askin questions and tryin to build what i could

when i got my own place i was almost thirty
went out to john barker's store one day to get supplies
that's where i met my wife margaret
she's a nice shape thing that stays in coveralls
hair cut so short you think she a boy
john ask about her and i tell him
she's tryin to get the garden goin
i get back to my place about three in the afternoon
john gave me a good deal
said it was the best wood i could get without goin
        down to the valley

well i start to unload this timber
and where john had it tied it came loose
and so the whole thing
give way and knock me down
i could hear the bone break in my leg
when the first piece of wood land on it
margaret come runnin from around the back of the
        house
her scream is like someone's gun bein fired in the
        woods

i try to get her to calm down and finally she does
but i don't know she ain't
my daddy once told me that some trees
got the devil in them
and when you go to hammer a nail
the nail breaks
and you stand there cursin the wood
unaware that someone
is listenin to you

you can tell bad wood just by rubbin your hand on it
or when you cut it and it don't smell good
i took some of john's lumber and built a fence around
margaret's garden
that was two months ago
you can go out there yourself
and won't see nothin growin
I tell margaret it's the wood makin everythin die
she said that's nonsense
well i wish my daddy was alive to tell her otherwise

a walk in the daytime
is just as dangerous as
a walk in the night

a simple dirt road
surrounded by all these mountains
trees and lakes
does not offer calmness
to my soul or mind
even here in upstate new york
the stillness drives a fear
through my heart like mississippi
or history and i cannot walk
without hearing the barking of dogs
or the yell from some redneck
screaming "there he goes"
i try to accept all these things
as irrational fears that
i should enjoy this time in the
country to relax and be at peace
with myself and i am happy
to be out walking in the morning
on this road which runs into
route 28 near eagle lake
not far from the small town
where i plan to purchase stamps
and postcards and while
i'm walking along the highway
feeling good about the weather
and thinking about nothing in particular
two vans filled with people
speed by and disturb the quiet and call me
  "nigger"

and the peaceful walk is no more
and in the midst of all this
beautiful scenery i become a woman
on a dark city street vulnerable
to any man's attack
it is not yet mid-afternoon
but the virginity of my blackness
has been raped
and this is no longer
a simple walk into town
this is like every walk i have taken
in my life wherever and whenever
i have been alone and my fears are
as real as this dirt beneath
my feet

helen

sometimes after someone has hit a foul
the umpire will toss a new ball back to the pitcher
the pitcher will catch it   look at it   rub it
then toss it back and ask that umpire for a new ball
just the other night i'm making love to helen
and it feels strange
helen got her eyes all closed
she squirming and moaning
but you can tell she's thinking about someone else
i run my fingers down her back like i'm tracing
the seams on a ball

helen & martha

after i got his third letter
i decided not to write
didn't know what to say or not say
went by the house yesterday and saw his wife and kid
ask if she heard from him
"no he ain't wrote since he left" she said
and i'm sittin by the kitchen table playin with the kid
thinkin about my three letters
and why i got them and she ain't
she his wife and me i don't know what i am
men always give me problems and other people men
well they give me headaches
problems and headaches is like water in your basement
reachin for the first floor
since i come to blue mountain
i don't think about nothin but keeping my own business
and believe me somebody's man
ain't what i like to poke my nose into

martha & helen

she got the body i once had
the kind men look for in magazines
i know why he be chasin after her
and why she always here playin
with my kid like she tryin to
make up for what she done or what
she's thinkin about doin
i know all his lies and i'm
learnin hers   i bet she got a
couple of letters already
he tryin to keep her warm
like a cup of coffee he can
come back to

poem by the lake

the silence
so loud

i think about you
while the wind
whispers your name

over the water

E. ETHELBERT MILLER is a founding member and the current chair of the Humanities Council of Washington, D.C. and a commissioner for the D.C. Commission on the Arts and Humanities. He has served as a visiting professor at the University of Nevada, Las Vegas, as an associate faculty member of Bennington College, and as the Jessie Ball DuPont Scholar at Emory & Henry College. Miller has won several honors, including the 1995 O.B. Hardison Jr. Poetry Prize and an honorary doctorate of literature from Emory & Henry College. Miller is the editor of several anthologies, including *In Search of Color Everywhere.* His memoir, *Fathering Words: The Making of an African American Writer*, was published in 2000.

E-mail: emiller698@aol.com / www.eethelbertmiller.com

Photograph by Mark Cohen

OPEN HAND
PUBLISHING, LLC

Other books of poetry
from OPEN HAND PUBLISHING, LLC

STONE ON STONE
(Piedra sobre Piedra)
Poetry by Women of Diverse Heritages
bilingual English/Spanish collection
edited by Zoë Anglesey

OLD WOMAN OF IRISH BLOOD
by Pat Andrus

NIGHTFEATHERS
by Sundaira Morninghouse
illustrations by Jody Kim
Children's poetry with soul

For more information on these books of poetry
as well as the complete current list of offerings from
Open Hand Publishing, LLC, please visit our Web site:
www.openhand.com